Croff

I

Fragile

Dedicated to my gorgeous lady, Sharon

Fragile

Geoff Thompson

Geoff Thompson Limited.
PO Box 307
Coventry
CV3 9YP
United Kingdom

www.geoffthompson.com

ISBN 9780956921543

Printed and bound in Great Britain by 4edge Ltd.

Note:

This play may not be performed without written
permission from the publisher. Please write to the above
address if you would like to discuss obtaining a licence
to perform it.

Design and Photo Credits

Thank you very much to **Owen Billcliffe** for his generosity in allowing me to use the cover image of Craig Conway.

www.owenbillcliffe.co.uk

Big thanks to **Oyster Design & New Media** also, for allowing me to use their amazing cover design.

www.oyster-design.com

Thank you also to my son **Louis Thompson** for producing the transcript, lay-out and design for this book and for my web sites.

www.coventrywebdesigner.com

Special thanks to:

Titas Halder, who brought me into the Finborough Theatre and helped me to develop *Fragile*.

Nick Bagnall, who was the inspiration for *Fragile* and who was instrumental in chiselling it into an amazing piece of theatre.

To **Kathy Burke,** who always champions my work and who first introduced me to Nick Bagnall.

Massive gratitude to **Debi Allen** (the best agent in the world – really), who encouraged me so much with this play and actually, incredibly, used her own money to help promote it.

Thanks to **Bradley Walsh** for being so generous with his time, and reading *Fragile* in London when it was still raw.

To **Hamish Glen** for bravely giving us space at Coventry's Belgrade to produce our play.

To **Craig Conway** for acting the words so sublimely.

Thank you to **Graham Baird** (Deputy Stage Manager) and **Hannan Finnegan** (Assistant Stage Manager):

these two amazing people made the unfolding of this production an amazing experience.

Thank you very much to **Ruth Saunders** at the Belgrade, who was massively generous and tireless in promoting *Fragile* and also in helping me to put this book together.

Thank you to all at the **Belgrade Theatre Coventry** for graciously allowing us to perform our play. It has been wonderful to work with such giving and professional people.

The Belgrade Theatre Coventry Presents

FRAGILE

By Geoff Thompson

Performed by Craig Conway

PRODUCTION TEAM

Geoff Thompson: Writer
Nick Bagnall: Director
Nicky Bunch: Designer
Mike Robertson: Lighting Designer
Peter Rice: Sound Designer
Steve Cressy: Stage Manager
Graham Baird: Deputy Stage Manager
Hannan Finnegan: Assistant Stage Manager
Set and Costumes made by Belgrade Production Services
www.belgradeproductionservices.co.uk

Photos of art works by Juan Munoz featured in *Fragile* are:
Pre-set: Conversation Piece

Act II: Towards the Shadow
Act III: Figure Hanging from one Foot
All by Juan Munoz. © Juan Munoz Estate

Extended thanks to:

Kevin at John E Wrights
Mick at Over the Moon picture framers
Candice McCann at Nuleaf Florists
Picture Frame Express
Liam McGuinness
John Bearmore

Fragile premiered at the **Belgrade Theatre, Coventry from Sat 8 to Sat 22 September 2012 in the B2 auditorium.**

Geoff Thompson
Writer

Geoff Thompson is a BAFTA winning writer and member of the prestigious Royal Court Writers Group. He has written forty books (published in 21 languages), five multi-award-winning films, three stage plays and hundreds of articles, many of which have been published in national magazines and broadsheets.

Geoff's autobiography, *Watch My Back*, was adapted into the major motion picture, *Clubbed*. It premiered in London's West End and Paris and was nominated for a BIFFA award. He has also adapted his first novel, *Red Mist* (Violent Heart, optioned by SteelMill Productions, London), into a feature film for cinema.

Geoff's third feature film for cinematic release, *Romans 12:20* has been optioned by The Tea Shop & Film Company in London.

Geoff lives between Coventry and Islington in London.

Nick Bagnall
Director

Nick is joint Artistic Director of The Milton Rooms,
Malton.

Theatre credits include:
Betrayal (Crucible Theatre, Sheffield); *Les Liaisons
Dangereuses* (Guildhall); *A Separate Reality*
(Royal Court); *By Jeeves* (Landor); Billy Liar (West
Yorkshire Playhouse); *A Midsummer Night's Dream*
(Milton Rooms); *Guys and Dolls* (Arts Theatre
Cambridge); *Entertaining Mr Sloane* (Trafalgar
Studios); *Burning Cars* (Hampstead Theatre); *The
Electric Hills* (Liverpool Everyman); *Mongoose*
(Assembly Rooms, Edinburgh); *Promises & Lies*,
Bolthole and *'Low Dat* (Birmingham Rep) and *The
Ruffian on the Stair* (Old Red Lion).

Future work includes:
Alison!: A Rock Opera (Kingshead Theatre) and
Henry VI Parts 1, 2 and 3 (Shakespeare's Globe).

Craig Conway
Actor

A founder member of the Northern Stage Ensemble,
Craig Conway has worked on stage and screen over
the last two decades. He is one of the company

directors and producers for Liquid Noise Films and Liquid Noise Films North with Lionel Hicks. He is looking to shoot the Sci-Fi Horror film *X-BREED* with Director Rob Green later this year.

Craig has written and directed for the Contact Theatre Manchester with *Freefall*, *Car Trouble* and was also Assistant Director for Richard Gregory's *To You*, the opening performance for Salford's Lowry Theatre. Craig has worked with Geoff Thompson previously, playing Malky in *Romans 12:20* and in the one man show *Doorman/Bouncer*.

Theatre credits include:
Animal Farm, *1984* and *Homage to Catalonia* (Northern Stage Ensemble) and *East* and *Macbeth* (Leicester Haymarket).

Film credits include:
Vera Drake (Les Films Alain Sarde); *The Tournament* (Mann Made Films) and Neil Marshall's *Dog Soldiers*, *Descent* and *Doomsday* and he has produced on *Devils Playground*, *FOUR* and *January* which is due for release later this year.

Television credits include:
Our Friends in the North (BBC); *Wire in the Blood* (ITV); *Eternal Law* (Kudos Film and Television), *Vera* (ITV); *Hogfather* (BSkyB) and *Inspector George Gently* (BBC).

Nicky Bunch
Designer

Training: Central School of Speech & Drama.

Recent design credits include:
The Taming of The Shrew, *Macbeth* and *As You Like It* (Sprite Productions); *Shiverman* (Theatre 503); *Les Liasions Danegereuses* (Guildhall School of Music & Drama); *Aladdin* and *Cinderella* (Hertford Theatre); *When Did You Last See My Mother* (Trafalgar Studios); *The Vancetti Sisters* (Tristan Bates Theatre); *The Long Goodbye* (Hampstead Theatre Studio); *The Archbishop and The Antichrist* (Costumes, Soho Theatre); *Guys & Dolls* (Cambridge Arts Theatre); *Artist Descending the Staircase* (Old Red Lion); *Macbeth*, *Ajax* and *Skull of Connemara* (Riverside Studios); *Well* (Apollo Theatre, Shaftesbury Avenue); *Steel Pier* (Mountview); *Oliver Twist* and *La Ronde* (Greenwich Theatre and Tour); *Frankenstein* (Sheffield Crucible and Tour); *Loyalties*, *I-Witness* and *The Lower Depths* (Finborough Theatre) and *Playboy of the Western World* (Riverside Studios and Tour).

www.nickybunch.co.uk

Peter Rice
Sound Designer

Previously Peter has worked as Senior Sound Technician at the National Theatre in the Olivier and as Deputy Head of Sound at the Royal Exchange Theatre in Manchester, where he designed the sound for over 25 productions as well as corporate work for George P Johnson, Aspect, Flourish & Blitz. More information on Peter's work can be found at www.peterricesounddesign.co.uk.

Recent theatre credits include:
Black Roses – The Killing of Sophie Lancaster (Royal Exchange Manchester); *Thoroughly Modern Millie* (Watermill Theatre, Newbury) and *Manchester Lines* for the Manchester Library Theatre Company.

Other theatre credits include:
Wind in the Willows, *Radio Times* and *Treasure Island* (Watermill Theatre, Newbury); *Hard Times* (Library Theatre, Manchester); *Saturday Night & Sunday Morning*, *Beautiful Thing*, *A View from the Bridge*, *As You Like It* and *Lady from the Sea* (Royal Exchange Manchester); *Winterlong* (Soho Theatre); *Cinderella* (Liverpool Playhouse); *Lady In The Van* and *Punk Rock* (UK National Tours) and *The Kitchen* (National Theatre – associate sound designer).

Mike Robertson
Lighting Designer

Winner of the 2007 Olivier Award for his lighting of *Sunday in the Park With George*, Mike is also a Whatsonstage.com Theatregoers' Choice Award nominee for On the Waterfront.

He has just created the 'New Colour Blue' series for the global Lee Filters range and has many West End and regional credits, together with international work in Norway, Sweden, France, Germany, Zimbabwe, Hong Kong and Spain through his practice Lighting Plan.

Recent theatre credits include:
Volcano (Vaudeville); *Death and Gardening* (Tour); *Six Actors In Search Of A Director* (Charing Cross); *Riccardo Primo* (Royal College of Music); *Rockin' Horses* (Playhouse Theatre, London); *Murder on the Nile* and *Funny Peculiar* (National Tours); *Cinderella* (Les Ballets de Monte-Carlo); *Third Floor* (Trafalgar Studios); *About Bill* (Landor Theatre, Clapham); *Fascinating Aida: Cheap Flights* (UK tour); *Oedipus* (Edinburgh Playhouse, Liverpool Playhouse and Nottingham Playhouse); *The Proceedings of That Night* (Pleasance Theatre, Edinburgh); *Cabaret* (Wilton's Music Hall, London); *Company* (Southwark

Playhouse); *By Jeeves* (Landor Theatre, Clapham); *Verdict* (National Tour); *Billy Liar* (West Yorkshire Playhouse); *Lark Rise to Candleford* (National Tour); *Biblical Tales* (New End Theatre, London); *Caroline O'Connor: The Showgirl Within* (Garrick Theatre, London); *Miranda* (Edinburgh Festival); *Legacy Falls* (New Players Theatre, London); *Guys and Dolls* (Cambridge Arts Theatre); *Du Ska Få En Dag I Mårå* (Norwegian Theatre, Oslo); *Jack* and *My Fair Lady* (Cambridge Arts Theatre); *Wolfboy* (Edinburgh Festival); *Too Close to the Sun* (Comedy Theatre, London); *New Boy* (Trafalgar Studios, London); *The Murder Game* (King's Head Theatre, London); *Hair*, *Deathtrap* and *Five Guys Named Moe* (English Theatre, Frankfurt); *Sandra Bernhard* (Manchester Opera House); *All Bob's Women* (Arts Theatre, London); *The May Queen* (Library Theatre, Manchester); *Whatsonstage. com Theatregoers' Choice Awards* (Prince of Wales Theatre, London, and Lyric Hammersmith); *The Marriage of Figaro* (Shaw Theatre, London); *On the Waterfront* (Nottingham Playhouse, Edinburgh Festival and Theatre Royal Haymarket); *Nonsuch* (St John's, Smith Square, London) and *Educating Rita* (Watermill Theatre, Newbury).

He was part of the team that designed the lighting for the new fleet of Virgin Atlantic aircraft, before going on to work with Airbus Industrie and designing the lighting for their Airbus A380, the largest passenger plane to date.

In addition to another 400 theatre and concert credits, Mike has lit hundreds of events for blue-chip companies including Wickes at the Ideal Home Show, which won the Best Design Award at Earl's Court.

FOREWORD

Fragile took me only two mornings to write the first draft. Manifesting the words on page was rapid, exciting and relatively painless.

The percolation period however was a different beast: it took forty years. It was neither painless nor was it exciting.

This material has been begging for expression since I was 11 years old. And for the last four decades I blocked its outlet, I forbade it form, and I pretended for a long time that it did not even exist. I did this because... *I was terrified*. I hid it because I was deeply ashamed. And I held it back because I did not know how to help it out; I had not yet built a strong enough conduit to deliver this ocean of raging emotion.

At times, my *beautiful Frankenstein* found its own surrogate exit, in spills of physical and sexual self-harm, in waves of crippling insecurity and in a ten year gush of violence – against myself and against others.

My insecurity was hidden from the world (and for a while hidden from me) beneath an array of

Heidelberg scars, garish tattoos and a plethora of Freudian Defense Mechanisms.

For the longest time I did not know who I was.

I was a house divided against itself, destined only to fall.

It was only after many years of academic, religious and *self* study, and many more years of sporadic living – a bi-polar existence that swung from *knowing* that I could change the whole world, to doubting that I could change my own socks – that I was able to find out who I really was, or more specifically who I was not. Once I'd discovered myself (hidden below layers of referred emotion) and taken back sovereignty of my life, I was able, at last, to find the courage to write *Fragile*, a play that Craig Conway so completely and so beautifully embodied on stage at the Belgrade Theatre in Coventry, and that Nick Bagnall so intuitively and so deliciously directed.

I was sexually abused when I was eleven years old. I first wrote about it in a book called *Watch My Back*. Since then I have had letters from hundreds of people from around the world – inspired by my honesty – with similar tales. This play then, is not entirely autobiographical; rather it is a myriad different stories that I have unashamedly weaved together into one narrative.

In the writing of this piece, I was determined not to embellish the subject in any way; The Initiating Abuse, The Secondary Abuse (family denial), The Ultimate Abuse (abandonment by God/our Source), the shame, the guilt, the possessing fantasies and the self-abuse are all factual.

There is no need to add fiction when the truth is already shocking enough.

Most people who are abused become emotionally crippled as consequence. Some never recover.

I refused to let this happen to me. I simply refused.

I changed my perception of the experience. I recognized that the fathoms of bubbling emotion in me, nine layers deep, was a potential reservoir of energy that I could turn into blocks of pure gold.

I have a prolific output, in books, films, plays, articles, talks and in life – I live the most wonderful life.

This is not despite what happened to me, rather, it is because of it.

I hope that in some small way, our play, these words, my unveiling will create an allowing in others to escape the shame disease by shedding light on their own shadows.

Thank you for taking the time to read *Fragile*.

(My next play is going to be a situation comedy – *I promised my wife*)

Geoff Thompson

Character

ONE – forty, built, confident, articulate, erudite....
cripplingly insecure.

Place: Anywhere/everywhere.

Time: Now or then (more or less).

Set: A dark unfurnished room (other than a table, a
Munoz picture, Conversation Piece, on the wall and
a tape recorder) that lightens and furnishes more
with each subsequent act.

SCENE ONE

A black room. Three black walls.

*On the back wall, a large picture, **Conversation Piece** by Juan Munoz.*

The back wall also has a black window covered by a black curtain. No light getting though.

ONE is dressed in depression-black. He is pacing. Slowly.

There is a tape recorder on the floor, sat on top of a silk towel, at the very front of the stage.

He is pacing and agitated.

He stops and looks at the tape.

Tentatively he walks over. He kneels down. Contemplates the recorder. Eventually he leans forward and presses RECORD.

ONE

One, one two....one two three....

He presses STOP REWIND PLAY and listens.

ONE (on tape)

One, one two....one two three....

He presses STOP REWIND and then RECORD again.

One clears his throat.

ONE

I'm special. I am. I'm very special.

Beat.

That's what he told me. He told me I was special. *Very* special.

Beat.

Everything that happens to me is good.

One stands up, steps back and paces.

It's about....perception. Perception...in Zen right... in Zen they say that you create your own reality. *You* create it. You create it so you can re-create it. Or change it. *Apparently.*

Mexican Shamans – listen to this – the Shamans actually collect their power from difficult situations, did you know that? Challenging situations. Their god is not some deity in the sky with kind eyes and a beard their religion is *experience* hard won – the harder the better. They collect their power from trauma….

Beat.

Rumi – he was a Persian mystic – he wrote about yokes that actually went out into the night and hunted down their fears – night travellers he called them – he even banged a chick pea into a pot and boiled it alive *so that it could be sweet, so that it could sit with the rice and the herbs*, just so's he could write an allegory about how pain is very good for us, about how pain is the necessary pre-curser to joy. And massive pain – you'll like this – *massive pain* is the dark night of the soul that comes just before revelation….thank you very much. Not every day you get council like that….not every day you're instructed to go out into the night and hunt for a little agony, 'oh love, when you're at Morrison's this week picking us up me beers and me Ben and Jerry's bang a bit of *excruciating pain* in the basket for me would you….do you mind…I think it might be on special buy two get one free?'

And Psychologists – wrap your head around this baby – this is what the depth psychologists have to say on the issue….*if you can change your perception to the bad things that happen to you… bad things…then the bad things that happen to you can become the grist for a happy life.* Like an alchemist turning all the shitty, leady, abusive, penetrative, traumatic, confusing, *excruciating* experiences into bricks of pure gold.

What you think about that then? What an amazing world we live in.

The Buddha – here's another I've got a rake of these – the Buddha, he's sitting under a banyan tree, having eschewed wealth and privilege and fine wine and women – he eschewed the whole jolly issue because before his enlightenment – and this is not widely known – before the large epiphany under a banyan tree he was a very wealthy man – the Buddha with his round belly digesting the problems of the world, our problems, digesting them for us, the Buddha living off the kindness and generosity of ordinary people, he said – and this is the fruit of a life time's pilgrimage…. he goes *life is hard*.

Is that it!

That all you've got to show? Well there's a shocker life is hard, talk about understatement, talk about stating the obvious that's like saying the shirt on my back is depression-black tell us something we don't know my fat friend. He goes – and this is what's been past down as scripture, this is what has been passed down as law – he goes 'only by accepting that life is hard can we transcend pain.'

Pain!

Apparently….it is good for us.

Beat.

Freud reckons that everyone is searching for comfort….not just me….but there can be no growth in comfort *can there*?....just fat birds... fat comfortable ladies….big heel-breaking wobbly lasses munching fish and chips outside late night take aways in perished leggings.

Beat.

I love that don't you, those programmes on the telly about big fat people being happy to be big and fat what a load of bollocks….they're not big and fat and happy they're just big and fat, big and fat and in denial who was ever big and fat and happy when was the last time you ever saw a big fat bird that was happy with their swaggy hips and their dangerously big wings swinging and knocking cups off tables? Big and fat and sweaty-depressed is what I see….my mum agrees – she's deliciously blunt my mum.

Beat.

Everything that happens to me….is good.

Beat.

Lord Krishna – you've seen his followers. On Oxford street, genie trousers, Nike trainers, shaved heads and moronic smiles (he sings Hare Krishna), banging tambourines (he sings Hare Krishna), singing to no one who is listening – Lord Krishna – the Godhead – he's riding to battle on his chariot with Prince Arjuna – not sure what he would have made of the Oxford Street Massive – he's riding into battle – this is in the Bhagavad-Gita – beautiful shell-blue face, long-bow drawn, quill of arrows over his shoulder, shield in hand, they're galloping into the battle of Kuruksetra. His kingdom has been stolen and he is going into battle to win it back. Arjuna is *scared*. He looks across at the enemy – a plethora, thousands of soldiers. All armed. The killing implements of war dripping red. He sees his friends, he sees his teachers, he sees his sons and grandsons, he sees uncles, brothers, cousins in the ranks and suddenly…suddenly he loses the heart for a fight. *In common parlance his arse-hole went.* The Lord Krishna notices, he leans across, little God-head twinkle of knowing in his eye, he goes to Arjuna, 'they're already dead, their karma is written – do your duty'. Arjuna is still shitting it, he doesn't want to fight, he doesn't want his kingdom back, at that moment in time all he wants to do is run and hide in the forest and spend the rest of his life begging for food.

'The self is the self's only enemy' Krishna says 'the self is the self's only friend.'

War is good for us don't forget that. Small wars, big wars, the microcosm the macrocosm, cut by paper nailed to the cross, everything….if it happens to us it is good, if it does not kill us *so the theory goes* it only makes us stronger.

In the new testament the Nazarene – Jesus of Nazareth, the Christos, the son of God – he goes – he's telling this to the apostles, Mathew, Mark, Luke, John – there's a few more but they don't rhyme – the apostles, they've all written about this since, they've all preached the word – Jesus goes 'the kingdom of heaven is within….seek the kingdom of God and His righteousness and all things will be given unto you.' Came straight from the cross that. Dying for us *dying for me apparently* I didn't ask you to but thanks all the same. Nails through his wrists, feet bolted to the wood, a roman spear – *The Lance of Longinus* – buried in his side, resurrection, new life, but only after twelve hideously savage stations, only after the cross – everything that happens to me is good – you don't get that kind of inspiration from a self help book let me tell you.

One paces.

Why do we need self help anyway why can't we be happy as we are – the shops are full of books and tapes and bollocks on self help – animals don't need self help they just get on with it they just live my dog don't need self help, you don't see my dog scouring the Waterstones bestseller list for *How to Win Friends and Influence People* no you don't…

Beat.

… mind you… my dog can lick it's own bollocks… I probably wouldn't read so many books if I could lick my own bollocks probably never get me out of the bathroom.

Stops.

'They took abundance from abundance' – this is in the Upanishads, from the Vedas – 'they took abundance from abundance and abundance still remained.'

Beat. – paces – stops.

I mean, what is that all about?

Beat.

He paces.

One stops.

'You're special' he goes….little wink, large greedy hand slithering and groping over the plucked chicken flesh of my very young arse, insatiable fingers fumbling…through thin cotton protection hunting….my virginal 11 year old willy exposed. It wasn't even a cock yet. It wasn't even a prick yet. It wasn't even sexual; it was something that I weed out of….it was my pissing tackle that's all, something that occasionally and of its own volition got erect when I was in the bath and my mum would say to me, 'you been stretching that again?'

'You're….different.' He goes to me 'you are different'…..his big trembling hand clumsy at the small buttons of my pyjama bottoms, flipping my young life apart. *Different.*

I was eleven. I was just a boy. I remember, I was
definitely eleven, just started big school, new
uniform, shiny briefcase, sharpened pencils, lined
exercise books with nothing written on the pages
yet, brand new shoes, I mean brand new, George
Best imprinted on the red sole – I was just perusing
along the outer edges of puberty, never seen a naked
woman before, never masturbated – that was soon
about to change – never had aspirations above
getting a love letter from Julie Beach and playing in
goal for the school team. She wrote my name in blue
ink across the knee of her jeans and I was Gordon
Banks for the first team reserves and that was better
than any sex to me. Eleven. He was a teacher. A big
man. Respectable man they thought, a good man
my dad said, he came down to the school 'specially,
straight from the working men's club – my mum
insisted – 'check the fella out' she goes 'make sure
he is solid, make sure he is safe' not the kind of man
that might spend an child-grooming year telling
their son how different he is, how special and then
shattering his life in one night of ultimate betrayal.

One stops pacing.

He was safe…my dad said he was safe – and my
dad was a nice bloke, I won't hear any bad about
my dad, he was a soft man ….he liked a beer but
he was a nice bloke, he came down to the school

'specially from the club, pissed in the teacher's toilet, pissed in the same troth – what do you think about that – the floor was slippy with piss I remember, they commented on it, I was there, 'slippy floor' said me dad 'piss slope' said the teacher, and they laughed and my heart leaped 'cus they laughed and that meant he was safe and I'd be able to stay over, me dad shook the teachers hand, nodded at me reassuring – I didn't need reassuring I loved the teacher, I idolised the guy, I worshiped the very ground that he walked on – my mum, she was the one that needed reassuring, she was the one that didn't want me away from her apron strings. And my dad did reassure her too. If there was anything untoward, he would have known. That's what he told her and that is what she believed. So I could stay over the night at the school. Help the teacher fix the damaged gym mats only as it turned out that there was no damaged gym mats…'sleep on the trampoline if you want to' he goes. *The trampoline*, I can't tell you how exciting that was to a lad that had only been in the world for 132 months *sleep on the trampoline* – 'or we could make a tent up for you in the gym – *how would that be?*' That would be spectacular as it goes, that would be very cool, and because I was different, because I was special, he said that I could stay in the same tent as him *but I shouldn't tell the other boys.*

Alarm bells!

I can see that now of course. I couldn't see it at the time but looking back: alarm bells!! I could stay in the same tent as him.
He was not safe.

Beat.

If my dad had come down to the school again, he'd have seen that. But if getting him out of the pub once was hard, getting him out twice would have been an ordained miracle….that's what my mum said. A miracle to get my dad leaning on anything other than the club bar. He was a nice man my dad. I loved him. I won't have any bad said about him. I loved his bones. I don't blame him at all…what more could he have done? He checked the guy out the guy checked out. Job done. My dad shook his hand, pissed in his toilet, came 'specially from the club just to do it… can't ask more of a man than that.

Did I tell you that I can kill a man dead with my bare hands. I can kill a man dead in twenty different ways all with my bare hands. There is bereavement in these lumps let me tell you, death; they can kill in sixty different languages from Coventry colloquial to Chinese Mandarin – they go through customs these. Look at me. Look. I'm built. I'm a lump. I'm

Sinewy. Svelte. A Marciano physique me – I'm forty with the body of a fit twenty year old. I am forty…I've spent a lifetime forging this machine, layer over layer, fold over fold, inch deep muscle, yard wide protection and I've spent my whole incarnation studying exotic killing arts. When I let these babies go it's a death sentence it's like a gun going off *and people fall over*. They fall, and they do not get back up again, it's a toe-tag with <u>your</u> name on it, a chalk outline and a marble bed guaranteed if I send these killers to work. Spent my entire existence searching for better, neater, nastier, bloodier ways of killing a man dead with my bare hands. The quicker the better. I could strangle you and you'd be dead before you even realised you was in a fight – oh the bliss the heaven. Arm round the neck, bicep into the right carotid artery, flexors into the left carotid artery and *squeeze*. Cuts the blood off to the brain. Ten seconds you'd be out like the gas, unconsciousness – varies a little bit from person to person but you *would be* out do not doubt me on that – twenty seconds brain death, if it didn't occur at birth – some of the people I've choked over the years were cerebrally *challenged* let me tell you, challenged,' Hold the strangle for thirty seconds and the bastards are dead, they are no more.

Beat.

And that is <u>my</u> choice…my choice not theirs.

Beat.

The power of life and death in these hands let me tell you. I could hack off your stealing-fingers with a world war two double-heel stamp and ram them up your hairy arse-hole see how you like it. I've travelled the world me, I've travelled the whole world, trained with elite forces, Olympians, street fighters from the back streets of Los Angelis, California, I've studied freestyle wrestling, Greco-Roman, Russian-Sombo, American Collegiate, Japanese Shotokan, Chinese Gung fu, Thai boxing, western boxing, drunken boxing, Brazilian Ju-Jitsu, African Copoera – I can kick elephants to death with these legs let me tell you – I could kill a horse with a single punch. I'm trained me. I am trained. I am trained in the art of the kill.

Beat.

Let me give you a snapshot from my youth;

One lays a blanket across the floor, kneels on it, as though he is with Julie Beach.

I'm kissing a girl in the farmer's field – not unusual, I'm thirteen I love girls…and girls love me…and I know what an erection is even if I am not entirely sure what to do with it at this moment in time in the field with Julie Beach – Julie Beach, my first love. I am thirteen years old and the innocence is bliss, like Eden before that apple – you can have too much knowledge you know, Eve proved that much. She is gorgeous – a tide of blond hair lapping down her back. I might only be a boy still but let me tell you I know what love is. I lean in to kiss her on the lips and I know she wants to kiss me back 'cus she's got my name penned in ink across the knee of her jeans. She is thirteen same as me and I have never liked a girl this much before never. I lean in for the kiss, my heart's hitting at a hundred miles an hour and I'm trembling when BANG!

He jumps up from the blanket and backs away.

Suddenly – and it was sudden, it was a shock I have to tell you, a shock – suddenly…it was her face…..
her face twists – that's the only way I can describe it – her face contorts into…it's like….it's a bloke's face a stubble-face and his thirty year old slug tongue is filling my throat filling it right up. She turned into a bloke and I jumped back with fright. And this ain't the first time it happened, it's happened a lot. Lately it's happening all the time. It's been happening ever since the tent thing…at the school….with the teacher…now I'm thirteen and I'm scared shitless of being alone with a girl again in case…..you know….
I mean I'm scared shitless of being alone, full stop.

Scared of what someone might do to me….scared of what I might do to myself.

Beat.

Another snapshot. I am eleven. Two years earlier. I am camping in a make-shift tent at the school, everyone is sleeping where they can, loads of kids, loads of teachers no mats to fix, 'the mats' as it turned out was a Trojan and it sneaked that hollow bastard into my confidence. It's safe. My dad even came down to the school to make sure. 'He can stay over', he told my mum, 'they're nice people at that school.' So I stayed over, I stayed over….as it turned out they were not so nice after all, that teacher, that lecher that leach, that monster in a people suit. It wasn't my dad's fault, how was he supposed to know. He did his level best, that's what he said, his best was not only his best it was his level best and he was thorough. He was thorough enough to settle my mum's mind, and mine was already set. Later that night – I'm the teachers pet so I get my own tent….I'm special. Apparently my idea of special and his idea of special were entirely different, and if I'd have known that then….well, if I'd known what special really meant and how being *special* was going to end my life I might not have trusted the guidance of my club-dad, I might have stayed at home in my own bed and never left my mum again. I definitely would not have begged her to let me camp out at that school because the other boys were. My tent was in a room all of its own, away from prying eyes, 'where things are not so cramped.' The teacher slept there too, and of course it felt a bit wrong but this is my first night away from me mum, I've only been on the planet half an hour, I've just started big school so pretty much everything is brand new to me and every experience feels *a bit* strange, I am not old enough yet to fully understand my own feelings. And anyway I trust him......actually...that's not true...that's not true I don't trust him trust does not even come into it, I idolise the man. I idolise him..... so I sink my instinct like a stone....it sinks and I pay for my folly....later. Later I pay for it...*I pay.*

Beat.

It happened when the night was coke-black....a hand....that was just the start of it – it got worse of course it got worse it always starts with the hand and it always gets worse... ....heavy uninvited – *uninvited* be clear about that – unwelcome fingers... pillaging.....

Beat.

My mum – I'll never forget this, it is branded here....on my warped drive – my mum she goes to me – this was after she found out, well…after I told her….I didn't tell her right away, it was years before I told her, the attention would have killed me, the attention would have mangled me, it would have hung, drawn and quartered me…I didn't have the protection at eleven for that kind of attention, I was soft still, I wasn't fully formed…I was just a boy… I hadn't developed the armour-light for that kind of *close scrutiny*, I only had my cotton pyjamas and they were not protection enough not nearly…. not to stop the kind of minds that search for fire at the first signs of smoke – and do you know what the copper asked me – I'll come back to my mum – the copper, when I was interviewed, when I finally found the bollocks to place the official experience in ink – I think I was about thirty when I found the courage to let a little of it bleed…had a rush of conscience 'cos he was still at large and other kids might be at risk – do you know what his first question was, the copper, the first words that dripped from his halitosis, a smug grin on his big butcher face, 'did you enjoy it?' And he's taping this, it's on a camera, in the police station, a small room, almost a cell, like I was the perpetrator – he's banging it on celluloid for prosperity, I wasn't sure if he was taking my statement or making a porn film.. Did I enjoy it? I was eleven years old you twat. Did I enjoy it? I was terrified… <u>I died a hundred years</u>… – and they still didn't catch him cus as it turns out you have to basically catch them in the act these paedophiles if you want to secure any kind of conviction so why was I even there, at the police station, writing my shame in black ink, thirty years old, on my second marriage, a head full of twisted grooming, a belly full of bad meat, a heart full of raaaaaaaaaaage twenty years after the event – and my mum, I was telling you about my mum – cus she told me not to stay over at the school, she warned me that it wasn't safe – my mum goes to me….she goes…. *(chokes a little)* she goes….*(clears throat – losing it)* and I still don't quite know what she meant to this day, not exactly, not entirely, not precisely, she goes *(bottom lip trembling)* 'you didn't lead him on……did you?*

One is choked – he clears his throat again.

What does that mean?

One starts to sob quietly.

'Did you lead him on?'

Louder sobs.

'You didn't…did you?'

Screams loud and long and from the bowels.

I was eleven years old. I was eleven mum, I was eleven I was eleven, I was eleven I was eleven.

Calms a little.

I was eleven for fuck's sake……

One *takes out a white hanky, blows his nose.*

I was eleven years old.

Walks to the tape recorder.

Looks at it. Breaths deeply.

Calms himself a little.

Listen to me mum listen….listen to me. I was eleven.

Beat.

I was a boy.

Beat.

I was ….I *am* innocent mum.

Beat.

I WAS A FUCKING BOY.

He angrily switches the RECORDER OFF.

SCENE TWO

Same room. Still black.

One hangs a new picture on the back wall.

*Munoz's **Towards the Shadow.***

There is a chair by the table.

He opens the back curtain, just a little, and allows a small crack of light into the room.

One sits at the table, he is still in black but his shoes are white now.

His hand is hovering over the RECORD button on the tape.

He holds it there for a long time.

He presses RECORD.

ONE

He's a story. You'll like this. A man, a man a man walks up to me – this is in the club, this in the working mans club, we go every Thursday, my dad plays darts, my mum plays bingo, everyone drinks, he is spastic drunk he is staggering and he's properly old probably can't see further than the rim on his pint mug but he comes up to me – it's Thursday night after the bingo, disco's on, everyone is dancing, my dad is leathered – usual – I'm at the edge of the dance floor looking for girls, middle of my family middle of my mates when bang! 'Can I have a dance?...*can I have a dance*? This is the old drunk guy. No you can't have a dance I'm a boy you blind bastard... I just looked at my dad, same age as this fella, same capacity for the drink, he goes, my dad that is, he goes, and he wasn't angry, embarrassed more than angry, puzzled more than angry, 'he's a boy' my dad says. The fella smiles, thinks my dad is joking, thinks he's having a laugh 'no, <u>he is</u> a boy' my dad goes, second time. The drunk makes a question mark with his eye brows – he makes a question mark, the penny drops and he slides off walking into a table of drinks, *ask me to dance thirty years on you old bastard when I'm built and you won't be tripping over a table of drinks you'll be wearing a table of drink*s – *I could use a table of drinks to kill a man dead I'm trained so jog on old man.*

Beat.

....so, so so so....large hand.... out of the burdock-night....yanks me out of my slumber.....it's rubbing and caressing my girly arse like a careful lover

– this is what I wake up to in the tent – like he's hoping to initiate sex – I am eleven and I know I keep mentioning the fact that I am eleven but it's important for me to remember that I was only eleven it is important that I keep mentioning that I was only eleven because people have the tendency, you have the tendency mum, you know you do, I know you do – even I have the tendency myself to think *no smoke without fire*, ...the bed of nettles, the scourging hand, the night terror and there is no care here, let us be in no doubt about that, there is no care, just probing fingers greedy....lusty talons groping.... a disturbed mind creeping – be sure of one thing....there was no care, not in his hand not in his dark intention, not in this oily black inferno of a night and not in the man that is about to alter the course of my very brittle life for ever and not for the better <u>and that is his choice not mine</u>....I am not a lover. I am not a potential lover. I am a child in the care of adults, the wrong adult and I am cold with terror and I desperately want my mum....

Beat.

....did I lead him on? You want an answer mum, you want an answer, you asked me this question a million years ago when I was too damaged to answer. Let me answer you now, not for you mum, not to ease your mind or to soothe your conscience, let me answer you now so that I can lose that bastard – so that I can hack that gargoyle out before I end or up swinging from the nearest oak myself. Let me answer you once and for all. Did I lead him on, bearing in mind that I was a child, did I lead him on bearing in mind that I had no idea what *leading on* even meant; I followed him around. I suppose I did that, I followed him around quite a lot. I hung on to his every word. I wanted to believe everything he said, because everything he said made me feel – that word again – special! I felt special. Who doesn't want to feel special? And when he said that I was special, with a nod and a wink and a nudge nudge of course I was thrilled, in my naivety I assumed that he meant I had potential, I dreamed that he meant I had potential.....just not the potential that he obviously hoped for, and when he said that I was different from the other boys, I thought he meant *different different* ...smart perhaps, top of the class maybe, an exceptional student....I didn't think not even for a millisecond, not even for the beat of a thumping heart that he meant *different*.

Beat. Gets his breath.

I'm in the tent. In that school. In that room hidden away....it's a make-shift throw together of a bed and I am sharing it with the teacher – I know, I know, I know, I know, it's thirty years on and I'm thinking 'how didn't you'….but I wasn't forty then, I didn't have four decades of life experience behind me, I didn't know how to kill a man dead with my bare hands, I hadn't been around the corners then that I've been around now, when you're that age you've been round no corners, when you're eleven you don't think like that, who thinks like that when they're eleven…..I'm in the bed…..I'm in the bed I'm in the bed I'm in the bed my little girly bony face, my pretty little bony arse, my delicate little bony hands my trusting little bony heart…six stone of child wheel locked to the bed ….did I enjoy it did I lead him on – I am leaden with sorrow that you could even ask – I am pinned to that bed like I'm nailed to a tree, I couldn't have been more trapped if I <u>was</u> nailed to a tree – I felt like I was nailed to a tree – my limbs are corpsed and terror is visited upon me in large chunks, big fear, too scared to cry out and of course I went straight to God, of course I did just as you'd taught me mum looking to be saved looking for salvation <u>looking for absolution!</u> Just as the priest told me at chapel, just as it says in the testament, but God was missing that night like you mum, God was missing that night like my dad, God was missing that night like my brothers, like my sister like everyone I knew like the rest of the world was missing presumed dead, God was missing presumed dead so fuck God – God did not come to my rescue so fuck him and you know what fuck the

Buddha – where was that fat beer-bellied preacher when you need him most he did not save me so fuck the Buddha and Fuck Jesus – did he save me? He did not save me so fuck Jesus and fuck Krishna that bruisy-blue wanker did not turn up when requested so he can fuck off and fuck Rumi, fuck the Shamans they can have their power and ram it up their ring piece I don't want it they can all fuck off….

ONE swipes the tape recorder off the table and it crashes to the floor.

….and you can fuck off as well…

Paces – points at the tape recorder on the floor.

And don't tell me that everything that happens to me is good. Don't.

Paces – starts to whine, like a child caught between and cry and a scream.

OOOOHHHH what am I doing what am I doing what am I doing I can't keep doing this I can't keep doing this, I can't keep doing this.

Talks at the sky.

Why are you doing this to me? What is this all for?
What is this all for? Answer me God you bastard.
Answer me!

One sits in the chair. Rubs his face.

He stands up.

SCREAMS into the sky with frustration.

Looks at the recorder on the floor.

Walks over to it…eventually.

He picks it up. Shakes it. Puts it back on the table.

*He reaches out and hesitates, his hand hovers over
the PLAY button.*

It stays there for a long time.

He presses play and listens.

The tape is stuck (from the collision with the floor).

It keeps repeating the same phrase over and over.

One looks on in fascination.

ONE – (on tape)

….looking for absolution looking for absolution looking for absolution looking for absolution looking for absolution looking for absolution looking for absolution looking for absolution looking for absolution looking for absolution looking for absolution looking for absolution…

He smiles at the irony.

He steps away from the table, away from the tape.

He tides around the room and straightens furniture as the tape continues repeating 'looking for absolution'.

He walks back to the table.

He presses 'stop'. He takes the tape out, looks at it; the recording tape is hanging from the case. He tightens it by turning his finger in the spool.

He puts it back in the recorder.

One presses RECORD again on the tape.

ONE – (deep breath)

One, one two, one two three.

One presses STOP REWIND PLAY and listens.

ONE – (on tape)

One, one two, one two three.

One presses STOP REWIND RECORD.

ONE

He took my <u>abundance</u> with his greedy cock that bastard…and nothing remains.

Beat.

You asked me did I lead him on mum. Stupid question. Wrong question. Stupid wrong thoughtless cunt of a question that I am not going to answer because I am *affronted*. Your questions are not my responsibility. Your guilt is not my responsibility. Your shame…. in fat leggings, eating chips, your comfortable…obese shame…..that certainly is not my responsibility.

Beat.

I've got my own shame to wrestle with without trying to strangle yours….

<u>My</u> shame. Let's talk about my voracious shame. Since it's been brought into the affray...since I brought it into the arena... let's talk about that....

Beat.

It needs to be....aired....it needs to be transferred... transferred to the tape....

Beat.

Not for prosperity....it need to be said because it wants to be out...I need it out...it is nailing me to a tree daily that blackmailing bastard.....it is murdering me.

Beat – One clears his throat.

I've got shadows....let's start with that shall we....let's start with my shadows and see what comes out...see what dribbles...she what spits....see what oozes..... shadows....I carry them around inside me...ghosts really.....haunting....old scars itching...screams muffled....grief denied....grudge throbbing like a cock looking for someone to pork.... raaaaaaage oceans of rage and guilt that thick, guilt wads thick. And I am full to the brim with shame....man I have so much shame...top of my hat to the toe of my boot wall-to-wall shame more shame that ten men and more voices in my head than I know what to do with. I am not congruent. *Not really.*

Beat.

I call myself a puritan – I call myself pure….I pride myself on it….*spiritually astute, karmically in credit.* I tell everyone *I've read all the big books* and I have read all the big books – but that don't stop me creeping in the dead of night….*hypocrite*…creeping when the lights are out and the family slumber – I am not so holy then let me tell you – sneaking and Googling….I am only ever two clicks and a spunky Kleenex away from nine circles of vice on the World Wide Web – all the wanking tackle a bloke could ask for at the touch of a mouse...and it's deliciously addictive. I am <u>not</u> congruent. I am not 'one'. I am not absolute. I am sharing this skin with too many faces, most of them I can't stand. I look in the mirror half the time I don't know who is looking back at me.

Beat.

….when you are traumatised at a young age – this is one thing I do know this is one thing I am certain of – when you are abused, when you are deserted, discarded, forsaken, dumped, neglected, cast off…. when you are cast off like shit on shoe, when you are kicked off like a mangy dog you develop an

Abandonment Schema. Schema....it's like a small growth – that's what the psychiatrist told me that's how he described it – a tiny growth on your perception but it only has to be that big *(shows tiny)* when you are eleven to end up that big *(shows big)* by the time your bollocks see hair. Come thirteen and that little blond kissing-girl in the farmers field will turn into stubble-faced-slug-tongue, a thirty year old man called Julie Beach who thrashes you with his thick purple root and spunks his dirty water in your face when you let him too close.

Long beat.

One smells his own hand.

I am forty....and I can still smell him on my hand.....

Beat.

... *everything* that happens to me is fantastic. Hard boiled, bone bad, difficult, very difficult, unbearably cruel, savagely inhuman....spiteful, mean, murderous angry, vengeful – apparently it's all fantastic....so why am I still wandering lost through the veins and arteries of this crippled bundle of bad influences?

Beat.

....if I don't do something with it....I've got to do something with it.... I've got to get it out.....I'll implode I know I will, I can feel it. And if it doesn't go in....if it doesn't burrow....it'll go out, it'll trickle, it'll spill, if I leave if for long enough it'll gush and when it does....when it gushes.....people will get damaged. People...have got damaged. I have damaged people. I have.

Beat.

So what do I want? What is the purpose of this? What do I want from you? What do I want from all of you?

Apology?

Dad? *Sorry for the abuse. I was <u>thirsty for a beer</u>, didn't mean to leave you unprotected. Sorry for the abuse.*

Mum? *Sorry for the abuse I was feeling <u>ashamed</u> I didn't mean to deny you. Sorry for the abuse.*

Teacher. What about you? What you got to say for yourself? What's your excuse is? *I was abused as a boy and I got sexual enjoyment from it, it taught me to put my own sexual enjoyment ahead of everything else, even you, a child in my care.*

Revenge. Is that what I am looking for? Revenge… revenge….sweet best served cold revenge…

When I crawled from that bastard school I didn't tell a soul.

My mind was warped…my trust was dead…I was too damaged.

Beat.

I wobbled through the next few years. Your brain is plastic when you're a kid, it's soft I was lucky enough to still have a mind I suppose but it was distorted, it was broken, it leaked….I didn't know how to fix myself there should be no cause to fix yourself at eleven. I was too ashamed to ask someone else to fix me in case …my slimy little story would have ended up on too many greedy tongues, …too noisy….people *know*…they know…they know that if there's a smoky abuse if there's smoke right, if there is smoke then some little cock gobbler lit the fire that caused it. Asking was out – so I turned in on myself … choking on my own soil. I started to self-abuse …I hurt myself…physically….sometimes I hurt myself sexually…..it was always violent.

Beat.

…Sometimes…it wasn't the anger that took me it was the….it was….lust…lust got hold of me ragged me around….got me by the scruff of the neck and dragged me…..bad places…bad places I didn't want to go…lust…. lust….it just comes over me, I could be just sitting there, I could be anywhere, I could be in company I could be with my wife and kids….I could be on my own…it was mostly at night, mostly when I was tired, usually when I was stressed and bang! Out the blue….it just hit me and…like I'm possessed, like another face takes over, like other hands take over not my hands….. *(choked)* ooooohhhhh it's hard to say this it's hard to say this….oooooooh noooooo it came over me and I'd…*(blows through his lips emotionally, eyes watering)*….I'd rape myself…I'd rape myself I'd rape….sometimes until I bled…just to get this….. just to get it out of me….anything phallic, finger, fingers, cudgel, truncheon, broom handle, the sharp end of the toilet brush would do the job, if it was shaped like a cock it was used like a cock – I pushed it inside me… digging my insides out, hacking my insides bloody out, and then the fantasies…. sickening fantasies….it was all….god it was all…. ohhhhhh no I don't like it…I don't like this I don't like this….get it out get it out get it out it was all fantasies of sucking and swallowing and licking and fucking, anal, oral, cottaging, frottaging, dogging, man….sitting on me….me sitting on their face, cock up my arse hole, cock in my gob, both at the same time, spunk up my crack, spunk dribbling from my mouth, rape, rape, rape, delicious rape, builders, policemen, strangers, teachers....

Stops – he has shocked himself.

.....teachers...

Beat.

Teacher.

Beat.

ONE looks at the tape...

His hand hovers over the STOP button...

He hesitates... he turns it off.

SCENE THREE

One hangs a picture on the right hand wall, Munoz's **Figure Hanging from One Foot.**

He opens the curtains, light pours in.

ONE sits on the comfy chair, feet up.

He is wearing more colourful clothes.

He presses record on the tape.

He sits back, he smiles, a big smile; his voice is calm now, measured, thoughtful and reflective.

ONE

(Mimics posh psychologist – " " denotes Psychologist).

"It is normal…your fantasy. It's normal."

Beat.

"Fantasy is just your mind – because it's been mangled, it's been… mishandled… it's just your mind trying to salvage something."

Beat.

"You should be thankful for it. If your mind hadn't found fantasy, if your mind had not escaped you might have ended up chewing on a wooden block and attached to the mains electric at the local mental asylum?"

Beat.

".....<u>you</u> have been impaired. Impaired....and it has left you exposed."

That's what he said, exposed. That is the word he used.

"Do you experience irritability or outbursts of anger?"

(irritable/angry) yes!

"....do you have difficulty concentrating?"

Could you...repeat the question....I...I drifted....

"....do you feel jumpy and easily startled."

Even the ring of a phone can force three shades of shit out of me.

"….Guilt, shame, or self-blame?"

In that order. In capitals. In italics. Underlined. In bold. With exclamation marks.

"….do you struggle to sleep?"

The days are *fucking* loooooong.

"….substance abuse?"

Yes please.

"….depression…..hopelessness."

I can fan letters from Prozac.

"….suicidal thoughts and tendencies?"

Thinking about taking in a West End show. Godot is on again….I've been waiting longer than Vladimir and Estragon.

"Post-Traumatic Stress Syndrome….that's what you are suffering from. Stress. Post. It's a traumatic syndrome."

….I read about it….what can I do?

"….anti depression tablets?"

How does <u>fuck off</u> grab you?

Beat.

I want someone to take my pain...<u>you're</u> a doctor….

"….have you read Siddhartha by Herman Hess?"

(One looks confused/incredulous).

Have I read Siddhartha – what kind of a prescription is that – I'm dying here?

Beat.

(Annoyed/irritable) Yes...I have read Siddhartha.

(Psychiatrist recites slowly, as a quote).

"….if you do not see a thing through to the end and conclude it then you'll have to meet the same situations all over again and all the same pains will have to be endured."

Beat.

....I don't know how to see it through to the end. I don't know how to get it out.

"....trick it out. Cry it out. Scream it out. Hammer it out. Coerce it out. Bribe it out. Threaten it out. Will it out. Imagine it out. Dig it out. Drag it out. Run it out. Intend it out. Climb it out. Train it out. Sculpt it out. Write it out. Talk it out."

Beat.

"Buy an old tape recorder and talk it out until it is spent. Talk until you are empty. A tape recorder is inanimate. It cannot point and whisper. It does not do guilt. It will not be tracing back the smoke to look for fire. It will not judge you. Tell it all. All the detail especially the seedy detail, specifically the seedy detail...the thoughts that hurt you most – get it out. *Every* detail. Nothing spared. To the very death."

Beat.

"......a tape recorder will not register your shame."

Beat.

I know that...I know...but I will......

Beat. – One looks at the tape recorder...

ONE

The teacher. The teacher the teacher the teacher...
even he....

Beat. – clears his throat.

....even that bastard finds his way into my head....
and each visit, each intrusion, each *possession* hurts
me more than the last because this time he is invited
against my better will but I invite him, me, I invite
him in but at the same time I loathe him. He is in
my fantasy that vampire in my shameful shameful
shameful shameful fantasy rolling out like a porn
film, and in it I'm needy, in it I am ready....I'm eager,
I'm hungry to be coerced, I'm happy to be fingered
I am begging to be fucked how's that for shameful
detail? Then afterwards – listen to this you'll laugh –
afterwards I am swept with regret, I am swept with
it, my mind is racked with the guilt, it's stretched...
it's tortured..... and I vow never never never to do
that to myself again, I vow it, I make it an oath,
I promise I pledge it and then....and then I spend
till the next time...and the next time, and the next
*time and the next...*bubbling under my skin with
self-loathing.

Beat.

My capacity to hate myself knows no bounds.

Beat.

Everyone *will* betray me. Everyone *will* abandon me.

Beat.

Why wouldn't they abandon me? I abandoned myself. When I was 11 years old, I abandoned me. *I...abandoned me.*

I've been abandoning myself every day since.

I don't trust anyone because I don't trust myself.

My trust is a skeleton... my trust is dry bones....my trust is buried in that tent back in 1981.

Beat.

I need to dig that poor boy up that's what I need to do. I need to lay out his poorly bones and put his body to rest once and for all.

Beat.

The police caught him you know. Thirty years too late but they caught him all the same – for a glut of historical abuses. On other kids – see I was not the only one he hurt mum, I am not my own....are all of us lying, did we all lead him on? And listen to this, the week before his day in court, the week before his victim's day in court...the very week before... he disappeared. Ran....to London. Papers said he watched a West End show, left the theatre, did his last meal then went back to his hotel room and hung himself by the neck from a door handle and I'd like to tell you that I was happy but I'd be lying because all I felt was sad...I felt *sad*. A life wasted....and a dozen abused kids one of them me trapped in their man-bodies with no closure.

Beat.

My mum – she's a pensioner now, she's a pensioner and her nerves are in ribbons. Her nerves are in the wind she's very old. I can't talk to her about this. I don't want to talk to her about this.....I can't talk to her about <u>any</u> of this she wouldn't cope.

Looks at the tape.

She's fragile.

Beat.

I have to handle her with care.

Beat.

I wouldn't hurt my mum. I'd rather swing below a hotel door handle that hurt her.

Beat.

I did try and to talk to her about it again…when the story reached the local papers. I said to her – and I had to corner her, she wasn't going to speak about my elephant in her front room, she'd even thrown the paper in the bin before I got there – I take her shopping on a Monday – I get there it's in the bin under a days rubbish! Like that's going to make it all go away, toss it in the garbage bag and it won't exist, *that was my teacher mum, that guy that abused all those boys* thinking it might open a discourse, thinking it might crack a little light through the curtain. She looked at me, like I was a boy again and I was crying tales about a wolf that didn't really exist, she said to me – and she was very stern, very direct, she glared, face twisted, ugly, disgusted….at me, disgusted at me – she said;

'….that did not happen to you!'

'…that did not happen to you.'

'....that...never happened to you.'

'...it never happened.'

'....you're a liar.'

But mum it did happen to me.

'......I told you never to bring shame to my door.'

'.....I will not have shame at my door.'

'.....it didn't happen.'

Beat.

'...that teacher was a nice man.'

That teacher touched me! He...touched...me!

I was eleven.

'....you must have....'

I was eleven! I'm lying on that bed, under his body, under his hands, his big eyes over me, his stubble scourging me, his slug tongue filling my throat I was eleven...

'…..your father went and met him….your father shook his hand…he made sure….'

My dad was pissed!!! He was pissed. He couldn't walk straight mum, he couldn't even piss straight mum, he wouldn't know a paedophile if one fell out of the sky and hit him on the head.

He slithered and piss-sloped with that yellow grooming <u>troth</u> of a man, he slipped his pissy fingers into the piss-hand that ripped my cotton apart how dare <u>you</u> mum…

'….get out…'

….how dare <u>you.</u>

'….go away from me now. I told you not to bring shame to my door. I told you never to bring shame to my door get out"! Get out!

Withdrawing your love mum. Running away mum. Pushing me away mum. Punishing me away mum? Hurting me mum 'cus you don't want to hear the truth. Hurting me mum! Like he hurt me mum, like dad hurt me mum, now you hurting me – how dare you hurt me! How dare you. HOW DARE YOU.

Beat. – gets his breath back. Softer now.

I love my dad mum I love his bones but he was
pissed. He was. Pissed.

Beat.

I was lying there....*(choked)* I was lying there,
crying and praying and begging inside my head
and all I kept thinking all I kept thinking all I kept
thinking all I kept thinking was – *I'm only eleven,
I'm not ready for this*, I was only a boy and I'm
not bothered about what he's doing to me, I'm not
bothered about what's happening to me – all I'm
thinking is all I'm thinking is *mum's going to be
so mad at me, mum is going to be so angry at me,
mum is going to be so upset, mum is going to be
so upset* and I kept thinking – screaming inside my
head, dying inside my head, running and running
and running inside my head – I kept thinking *I'm
sorry mum...I'm sorry mum...I'm really sorry mum
please don't be angry at me mum please don't be
mad at me mum please don't fall out with me mum
we haven't fell out have we mum please talk to me,
talk to me talk to me mum talk to me....*

PLEASE FORGIVE ME, MUM.

*One breaks down on his knees and sobs and sobs
and sobs.*

He gets up. Moves furniture, tries to place everything in its right place and in its right order.

I just want everything to be back like it was before but I know that everything can't be back like it was before because everything has changed and I don't know what to do with that I don't know what to do with that I don't know what to do with that and I am a boy and I am in the world and I am alone because I don't know what to do with that or who to talk to about that or even what that means I am alone.

Beat.

I am alone.

The tape suddenly ends. One looks flustered by this. He has more to say, more to purge.

He opens the cassette up, and takes out the tape. Looks at it. It is definitely full.

Beat.

He walks over to the large oak cabinet and opens it, looking for a new tape, a fresh tape.

Inside, the cabinet goes back further than seems possible.

The cabinet is jam packed with boxes of empty tapes.

He takes the boxes out. Searches for a fresh tape. He doesn't find one.

He opens the cupboard again, takeout more boxes and more boxes, an impossible amount of boxes, until finally he finds a fresh tape.

ONE – (to himself)

He took abundance from abundance…

He walks over to the tape recorder.

Puts the tape in.

He takes a deep breath (here we go again) and presses RECORD.

ONE

One, one two, one two three…

He presses STOP REWIND and PLAY.

He listens.

ONE – (on tape).

One, one two, one two, three...

He presses STOP REWIND and then RECORD.

One clears his throat.

ONE.

I'm special. I am. I'm very special.

Beat.

That's what he told me. Special.

Very special.

VERY SLOW FADE.

END

www.geoffthompson.com